How to Publish for Next to Nothing

By Ryan Griffin

First Edition: Oct. 2016

ISBN-13: 978-1-519-48258-7
ISBN-10: 1-519-48258-2

Front Cover Design: Pixelstudio found on www.fiverr.com

Back Cover Design: Digital Revolution

Printed in the United States of America

Published in Red Lion, PA, USA

Fans, haters, or interested parties with questions, raves, reviews or anything else may contact the author at griffincyde@gmail.com.

All information in this book is accurate as of the October 2016.

10 9 8 7 6 5 4 3 2 1

Disclaimer: All links, companies, brands, and software sited in this book is represented with the most honest intentions of the author and publisher. Ryan Griffin is not associated with any of the third parties sited in this book (with the exception of www.facebook.com/digitalrevolutionimaging, www.autumnshadows.webs.com and the "Central PA Local Author Network" Facebook group). Using any of these resources is optional and subsequently, the author, publisher, printer etc, cannot be held responsible for any negative outcomes, problems, or errors etc. in downloading or using these resources. Discretion and responsibility falls solely on the user of such sites and software and due diligence should always be utilized with any party, company, site, or software.

Additionally, no companies have sponsored, endorsed, or are affiliated with this book or the ideas expressed therein by the author, publisher, or printer.

This book is dedicated to the writer in all of us that maybe not all us acknowledge or encourage but that eternally strives to find its way to the surface anyway. I'd wish I'd had this book years ago when I first started wanting to write seriously and professionally. It would've saved so much time. However, my time spent is your time saved.

So who is this book perfect for? Anyone that is currently alive and can read. Those are probably the only stipulations for this book to be a perfect gift for everyone! They say everyone has at least one book in them. If you aren't going to tell your story, who is? Give it as a retirement gift to mom, dad, or a colleague. Give it to a graduate as congratulations, give it as a birthday present to your brother, sister, son, daughter, niece, or nephew. Give it to a friend after they've accomplished something extraordinary! Give it to anyone that loves to write and you will open up a world of creative possibilities...

Table of Contents

Factoid:
"PS" stands for "post script"
which means it's an add-on meant to
augment the main points of a letter.

1

INTRO

So you want to publish a book? More importantly, like me, you don't have a lot of funds to invest in this endeavor ahead of time but you still really want to publish a book... No problem, I'm going to show you a short and simple guide on How to Publish for Next to Nothing. In this guide, I will share all of my resources, knowledge, tips, & tricks on how to do just that. I consolidate all of this information to help you do what took me years to figure out how to do on my own.

A little background information on me before we get down to business. I grew up in southern York County, PA and went to public schools. I excelled in almost all areas of general education early on but lost steam in my early teens and my grades suffered. I was a product of lower middle class upbringing which basically meant, there was always food on the table, but I had to work for everything else I wanted. I did not enjoy nor thrive in high school and barely graduated despite having an above average intelligence. I was disinterested and threw myself into novels as a form of escapism. To me, there was nothing greater.

At 18, like so many others, I had no idea what I wanted to be or do when I graduated. I knew how little I enjoyed a general education and decided that college, at least at this point in my life, was not the best option. That only left so many other options to tend to, especially being lower middle class. Either get a job or go into the military. I coincidentally fell into contact with a Marine Corps recruiter and thought to myself "why not?" I basically enlisted into the United States Marine Corps on a whim.

Throughout my stint in the Marine Corps, whenever I found downtime, my nose usually found its way into a book. The Marine Corps, in all its elite glory, left a lot of us lonely or missing home. Reading was one small way to distract myself of being so far from home.

I had written my first poem "Autumn Shadows" in 1999 as an assignment for English class, which, ultimately, set the stage for my first book. It came out great and I was proud of it but had no idea it would lead to anything else or such a love of poetry.

However, in 2006, ideas just started coming to me, general topics and themes for poems and I decided to start writing them down. I would jot down ideas, topics, and short stanzas I'd thought up spur of the moment to develop them later. Sometimes, two different ideas for poems merged to become one and sometimes one idea read better when split up into two different poems. I started to study the work of such greats like Edgar Allan Poe (who is undoubtedly my biggest inspiration) and Robert Frost.

I wrote many poems from 2006 to 2009 and it trickled off after that with an occasional one here and there every few months. However my love of reading and writing overall never diminished and in 2012, I started looking for publishers online.

Google is a great and powerful thing. Technology and innovation have made it so much easier to do the things we want to do or to learn the things we wish to learn.

In my 20's I started to redevelop my love of learning, I learned about things I was interested in and things I didn't realize I would ever care to learn, like how the differential steering in a car works. I watched a video on it just because it was there and I was intrigued and had learned something completely new at the same time.

My whole point is that we live in a great era of technology and information. There was no internet when I was a kid and when we finally did get it; it was limited dial up connection with 100 total minutes of usage a month.

The internet and Google also allowed me to start learning everything I needed to learn about publishing a book and everything that goes along with it. Countless hours, over the years, have been logged into this process. I went to work, I came home, and continued to work on my craft, all to your benefit. I will compress everything that I have learned along the way into this short guide for you to accomplish your dream of having a book published just like I accomplished mine.

I came across numerous publishing companies that would essentially publish anything you wanted for the right price. I would later learn that many authors refer to these publishing houses as vanity publishing.

Back in the day you had to have an awesome manuscript and hope a company would listen to your pitch and consider it, then pick it up and help you publish and market it. This path of traditional publishing still exists but it can be pretty difficult to accomplish. Self publishing companies make it possible for anyone with the will and fortitude (and necessary funds) to write a book and to be published. I'd contacted numerous companies and had gotten on plenty of call lists but because packages ranged from hundreds of dollars into the thousands, I never made the jump.

Then I discovered www.createspace.com. This self publishing platform was completely free for all of the basic features needed to publish a real physical book. They offered pay options for extra features like professional cover design or a custom ISBN, but everything that I needed and wanted was free. I was able to print my books for next to nothing and I will show you how to do the same.

I'd dreamed of being published for years, my friends and family will tell you how often I'd talked of it, only to accomplish it after an extraordinary amount of effort. But it's possible. Not for everyone, not for people who kind of want to do it, but for those that are passionate beyond measure and are willing to work hard and put in the time and effort, here is your How-To guide (for next to nothing).

Factoid:
Stephen King writes for three to
six hours a day and tries to have a
finished rough draft in three months.

2

SELF PUBLISHING

This guide won't help you write a book, only to publish it, so assuming you've already completed that step or are close to completing it, where do you start? There's lots of ways to publish, I'm going to show you how I did it (for next to nothing) and the steps that I took.

There are so many self publishing sites in existence. Xlibris, Lulu, Author's Publishing House, iUniverse... the list goes on and on. Many of these sites however simply offer publishing packages ranging from a few hundred dollars to a few thousand dollars. They will provide you with services including cover design, editing, formatting, marketing etc. but if you're like me, then you are not quite there financially to be able to put forth that much money.

I recommend **Createspace** as that is the process this guide is geared toward. You can publish your manuscript virtually for free and simply pay per copy to print your books.

What's even more amazing (as a Print-On-Demand service), there is no overhead (stock) for you to worry about or store. They will print and ship each copy to it's buyer as it is purchased online (through Amazon or Createspace). I love the fact that I don't have to deal with the shipping & handling as well. Amazon takes a 40% commission on the sell price of the book (but they print it and save you the trouble of shipping & handling). Sounds fair to me. If a customer buys a copy directly from Createspace via your e-store, they will take a 20% commission. Keep in mind, they are doing most of the work and most brick and mortar (physical location) book stores will take 40-60% of the sell price. I'll touch more on this in Chapter 8: Distribution.

Much of what I write can be generally applied to other sites and print on demand services but this guide will be specifically for Createspace. Step number one is to create an account on www.createspace.com. Sign up, login, and complete the basic steps they assign to you.

Under **Member Dashboard**, all of your projects will be listed. They have numerous platforms that you can publish under. Paperback books, e-books (you'll follow the process of paperback books to accomplish this), Audio CDs,

DVDs, and Video Downloads. Then choose a **Guided** or **Expert** set up process.

I recommend 'Guided' for first time authors. The great thing about Createspace is that they show you everything that you need to do to meet their requirements for publishing a book from meeting technical aspects to choosing an ISBN (International Standard Book Number which I cover more on in Chapter 5: ISBN) to choosing a price and so on. (Well, if Createspace shows me everything I need to do, why am I reading this guide? Because I will tell you everything that Createspace does not tell you and consolidate countless sites, pages, and sources all into one place.)

Title Information
Under **Set Up**, your first objective will be to fill out all of the basic information of your book: title, subtitle, author's name etc. Don't worry if you don't have a final book title yet, you can always go back and change it before publishing. If you're unsure if you should include something or not in your book, look at how other authors within similar fields or genres present their book.

I have a modest library of roughly 350 books and I referred to them for numerous things like font, size, color, spacing, subtitles, back cover design, copyright page, etc.

Some people already have a title when they start writing a book and some people write a whole book and come up with a title at the end. Nothing wrong with either but I recommend before settling on a title that you do an Amazon search to see if it is already in use or that if you decide to use a kind of generic title like "How to Publish for Next to Nothing" that you search it as "How to P" to see if people are already searching for what you are offering.

3

COPYRIGHT & THE LIBRARY OF CONGRESS

A copyright basically protects your intellectual property from plagiarism and lasts for the entire lifetime of the author + 70 years, depending on the jurisdiction/country. Anything that you write is automatically protected by copyright as soon as you record it or make it "fixed in a tangible medium of expression".

Intellectual property (IP) refers to creations of the mind, such as inventions; literary and artistic works; designs; and symbols, names and images used in commerce.

IP is protected in law by, for example, patents, copyright and trademarks, which enable people to earn recognition or financial benefit from what they invent or create.

A work does not have to be published

anymore to be considered copyrighted. Publication simply meaning being made available to the public by way of sale, rental, lease, or lending. Although using the © symbol with your creative work isn't necessary, include it anyway as it serves to notify anyone that it is officially copyrighted material (and is protected under the law). As the owner of the copyright, you have the right to

- Reproduce copies of your work
- Display the work publicly
- Create derivative works based off your previous work
- Sell and distribute your work to the public
- Sell, lease, rent, or transfer the copyright of your work to others

And many other things as well. *All Rights Reserved* means just this, that you reserve the right to do with your work as you want.

What is protected under copyright?

- Literary works
- Musical works
- Dramatic works (like live plays)
- Pictorial (pictures and artwork), graphic, or sculptural works

- Motion pictures and other audiovisual works
- Sound recordings
- Architectural works

So what is not protected under copyright?

- Works that have not been fixed in a tangible form (written or recorded)
- Titles, names, short phrases or slogans, familiar symbols and designs, mere listings of ingredients etc.
- Ideas, procedures, methods, systems, processes, concepts, principles, discoveries, or devices (this does not include descriptions, explanations, or illustrations).
- Works consisting entirely of information that is common property and containing no original authorship (for example, standard calendars, height and weight charts, tape measures and rulers, and lists or tables taken from public documents).

The saying "the devil is in the details" applies here. While a list of ingredients cannot be copyrighted, a secret recipe absolutely can. So a list will tell you what ingredients a meal uses: pasta, sauce, water, salt etc. A recipe will include exact measurements and how or when to apply it and what temperatures to use etc.

Registering your book with the US Copyright Office (which is a dept. of the Library of Congress) is $35 if you file online ($85 by pen and paper). You must also send them two copies of your book. Sending a copy of your book or work to the Library of Congress simply makes it easier to prove the work is yours in a legal dispute.

The PCN or Preassigned Control Number Program is a way for authors to have their book given a PCN prior to their book being published so that US libraries are able to acquire it.

Createspace can help you get a LCCN (Library of Congress Control Number) for your book for $25.00. It's the same thing as a PCN but is acquired after you publish your book, should you want to donate any to libraries.

Www.copyright.gov and www.loc.gov/publish/pcn are great sources for copyright information. If you have a book of poems or short stories, I recommend putting them together in one book to copyright that way they are all protected but not individually copyrighted (and you can save on the cost of copyrighting each). The address follows:

Library of Congress
U.S. Copyright Office
101 Independence Avenue

SE Washington,
DC 20559

You do not want to use any images or work that is copyrighted without the proper license. To see if an image is copyrighted, you can use www.tineye.com or Google reverse image search. For the copyright page, I referred to several different books from my personal library as examples. They ranged in content a good bit, but most contained the title, the year published and copyrighted with author name, fiction books usually contain a disclaimer stating any names of characters matching real individuals is purely coincidental etc, author's reserved rights paragraph, First Edition month and year, 13 digit ISBN, 10 digit ISBN (if you wish to include that as well), cover design credit, back cover design credit, pictures illustrated by credit, country of print origin, a way to contact the author or publisher, usually a street or email address, and the Edition line.

Rarely will you find a professional looking book without most of these key elements. A dedication and acknowledgements section are nice but not necessary. Ahead is the copyright page for my book Autumn Shadows (with an explanation of what each is in a different font.

The All Rights paragraph is a legal liability waiver that says you are in no way trying to embarrass, defame, or slander anyone who shares a name or similar name or likeness (resemblance) with a character in the book. There are too many people and too few names in the world that some of them just happen to get repeated and reused from time to time. Nothing you can do about it other than post a disclaimer. Your author rights are inherent with any copyright or publication, this section just clearly states them for the education of others.

13 digit ISBN - International Standard Book Number, for tracking purposes just like a person's social security number, because books do sometimes share titles with other books on occasion.

10 digit ISBN - This tracking system is slowly being phased out due to the enormous number of books being published, some older systems do still use a 10 digit ISBN though.

Printed in the United States of America (Country of print origin. This isn't necessary but looks professional as many publishers do this.)

Most authors simply have the publisher's contact info: name, address, phone number, and email address but for self published author's I recommend using just an email and/or business cell number. I include this mainly for marketing purposes and for the benefit of sincere fans.

10 9 8 7 6 5 4 3 2 1 - This series of numbers just shows which print version of this edition that this book is. Small things like grammatical and typographical errors that are not caught before

the first print but are later fixed and reprinted. These numbers just help keep track of which book is which version. Remember, a new edition (which could be a hardback, ebook, audio book, limited edition etc) would get a new ISBN because it's a different enough from your original to matter to a buyer, however, the buyer typically doesn't have a say in what version of that edition they will get, they will simply get the latest one.

If you chose Createspace's free ISBN option, please note the following conditions:

- "CreateSpace Independent Publishing Platform" is the imprint of record for all books with a CreateSpace-assigned ISBN.
- If we assign your book an ISBN, you cannot use the ISBN with another publishing platform.
- Books with a CreateSpace-assigned ISBN are registered with BooksinPrint.com.
- A CreateSpace-assigned ISBN is required if you want to sell your book through the Libraries and Academic Institutions sales outlet through the Expanded Distribution.

Trademarks

No one else has the right to use your brand, logos, images, works, or copyrighted material except within fair use practices outlined in four different areas.

- Criticism or parody
- Educational purposes
- Transformative purposes
- Public Domain

No matter how scathing or distasteful a harsh critic might be, you cannot stop them from using your work and likeness, as doing so falls under Free Speech.

If someone uses your work for educational (and non-commercial purposes) it is usually allowed. Every case is different and there are so many variables that a judge will look at, so these really are just general guidelines.

If someone uses your original work and adds so much to it whether it's a parody or a completely new work, they sometimes are allowed to do so (especially if they do not hurt you economically or target your main audience). Again, another fickle condition to deal with but it's been done before.

Most copyrights run out after the life of the author plus + 70 years (there are some exceptions but overall, that's the golden rule). After that 70 year period, most works enter into the Public Domain, where any and everybody are free to use the characters, storyline, and exact original work as they please, privately or commercially.

Trademark infringement occurs when someone utilizes or misrepresents your brand, logo, slogan, name, or other affiliated trademarked aspects of your work with a similar product to the extent that it would cause genuine confusion among customers or potential buyers.

Trademark dilution is generalizing a brand instead of using it in proper context: "googling" vs. the proper "doing a Google search".

Below are several areas that can get you into hot water if you are not careful.

- Infringement
- Defamation
- Right of Publicity

Infringement is the clear and unauthorized use of someone else's works, likeness, or story whether through pirating, plagiarism, or theft etc.

Defamation happens through libel (being written down) or slander (verbally) and disgraces or damages the reputation or good name of another person (living or having lived and is now deceased) with false information or allegations. Everyone is entitled to have a good name and reputation and not have it falsely tarnished for whatever reason.

If the disparaging information is true, be prepared to show, not simply tell, the world because you could still be sued for defamation because you cannot prove what you said.

Opinions are also protected from defamation as long as it is expressed as such and not being passed off for truth. "The restaurant smelled moldy" vs. "the restaurant had mold."

If you complain publicly about a company or individual that you were unsatisfied with their goods or services, be prepared to show, not tell, what happened, as no proof might trigger a defamation lawsuit.

If someone else makes a false claim and you repeat it, you are equally as liable to be sued as they are because you continued the defamation.

However, information that is damaging and can be proven true is not defamation and can be published. Just make sure you have proof before making any claim. The only exception to this rule would be something that someone says or does in private (like their own home) and is published to embarrass or damage the reputation of said person by bringing to public light (like someone's sexual preference or what they wear to bed etc).

Casting someone in a bad light whether through negligence or direct malice is also an offense. You may not make someone out to be a criminal or deviant by linking them to someone else that might be etc.

The Right of Publicity (or personality rights) is the right of an individual to commercially control their name, image, likeness, or any derivative identifying marks (works they've done). You can't just claim a celebrity loved your book, that is a false endorsement and you could be sued for that.

As writers, we are naturally inclined to want to use our friends and relatives as characters in our book, however that is generally a bad idea as no one wants to be cast in a bad light. You should change enough facts about said person/basis for character that they and no one else can reasonably draw a correlation between the two. That means changing the name, style, sayings, and habits enough so that it really could be just about anyone.

All of my advice can be summed up by saying, stay out of the courtroom and stay working on your next book. You can help yourself by staying clear of blurred lines within these areas and if you think someone should happen to infringe on your copyright, decide if it's worth it to go after them. Sometimes a cease and desist letter from a lawyer will do the trick.

However if someone should happen to

use your work without your permission, you may use the Digital Millennium Copyright Act (DMCA) and send them a takedown notice. The Electronic Frontier Foundation (www.eff.org) helps writers and artists perform takedown notices.

And remember, I am not a lawyer or paralegal and should not be relied upon for actual legal advice. All of the information in this book is for general guideline purposes. Seek the advice of a licensed expert in the field you are looking for, for real world legal advice.

Factoid:
The use of three dots... in the middle of a
sentence is called an ellipsis. If used at the end of a
sentence, there are four dots (including the period)....

4

BRANDING YOURSELF

When you become a well known author, your name becomes your brand. Look at the biggest names out there: Stephen King, James Patterson etc, their names are splayed across the entire width of their books and that's because their name is their brand. You must brand yourself as well. Business is good, but repeat business is better. If your readers enjoy one of your books, they will most likely purchase more. Create a reputation for yourself by being an excellent author then create a brand by marketing yourself as an author of a specific genre (I decided to brand myself as an author that writes dark poetry and fiction.)

Some authors use a pen name* when they publish a book because they step outside of their usual known genre. Stephen King has done it.

Recording artist Garth Brooks has done it and many more have as well.

*A pen name is just a different name you publish a book under in order to differentiate yourself from your normal brand or genre. Authors and artists do this because their followers expect a certain theme or style and authors don't want their followers to be disappointed by receiving something they weren't expecting. Thus, the pen name. A new name means a new style.

Having a unique one liner to write when signing books is a nice part in branding yourself. For Autumn Shadows (a dark poetry anthology), I usually write their name, "Beware the Shadows", and then sign my name. Sometimes I'll thank them for their support etc.

Fonts matter!
The type font for your cover helps set the tone and genre of your book. Again, I'll refer you to look at covers online and in your own book collection. Different genres (should) depict feelings in the reader. Horror and thrillers are often big and bold, with slime, blood, thorns, or other details. Romance fonts tend to be thinner and more flowing (somewhat like a cursive font).

5

ISBN

ISBN stands for International Standard Book Number, which is how book stores, online retailers and distributors track your book properly. Every book has its own ISBN, if you publish a paperback and decide to later publish it as a hardcover, e-book, audio book etc, you will need another ISBN for that new version.

Customers and retailers need to distinguish one form from the other and know what they are ordering. ISBNs used to only be 10 digits long, however now, they are 13 digits long to accommodate a growing industry.

ISBN sellers will usually give you a 10 digit and 13 digit ISBN for you to use in conjunction with your book depending on your needs as the author or seller of the book. The 10 digit ISBN system is slowly being phased out and eventually all books will use a 13 digit ISBN. You need to put your 13 digit ISBN on the back cover and copyright page of your book (if you want to be able to sell it in stores or in a more official capacity than say a yard sale); the 10 digit ISBN is optional.

Createspace will give you both, a 10 digit and a 13 digit ISBN, and has 4 different ISBN options. I chose and recommend the free option which means they will issue you an ISBN for your book; however you may only print this edition through Createspace and not another publisher.

With the $10 Custom ISBN option, the publisher assigned to your ISBN is your imprint. The ownership and authenticity of all ISBNs and imprints are verified. If you elect to sell your book on Amazon.com, the imprint will appear on your Amazon.com product detail page. If you use a free CreateSpace-assigned ISBN, "CreateSpace" will be the imprint for your book. With the Custom ISBN, your imprint can be whatever you want, like the name of your own publishing company.

The $99 Custom Universal ISBN option is designed to give the author full flexibility over this edition of the book that can be printed through other publishers if the author chooses. Basically you buy your custom ISBN from a verified third party and you use it with whatever publisher you choose, in this case; Createspace.

The "Provide Your Own ISBN" option is if you have already purchased an ISBN from a company for the intended use of your book but simply haven't published it or found a publisher yet. Most ISBN issuers will sell blocks of ISBNS for a bulk discount price. Sometimes a nice option if you plan on publishing a whole series, however, I would still prefer to use CreateSpace's free feature even for a series, this is after all how to publish for next to nothing. Our focus is on publishing for as close to $0 as possible. Whatever you decide to invest in your book is completely up to you however.

Bowker offers lots of paid for services as far as ISBNs and cover designs etc at www.myidentifiers.com.

The first 3 digits of the 13 digit ISBN are the EAN (European Article Number or International Article Number), Group Identifier, Publisher Prefix, Title Identifier, and Check number.

Factoid:
John Grisham writes and publishes
an average of 1.3 books a year.

6

ANATOMY OF A BOOK

Next is **Interior Options**, such as what type of paper to print it on and whether it will be black text with the option of black and white pictures or with full color photos and also **Trim Size.** Full color photos can only be used in conjunction with the white paper option.

Look inside a few of your books to see the author's choice of font, text size, margin, title or chapter number place & size, and general design or check out www.bookdesigntemplates.com for some ideas on a good book layout.

Different options will lend a different feel or tone to your book. Consider what you are going for and see how it compares to some of your favorite books of a similar genre or book type. To me, cream colored paper is more Earthy, more personal, more character driven, while white paper is more formal or academic like what would be used in a college textbook. Remember to balance what you want with what you think your typical customer will look for when picking up your book or browsing it online.

Trim Size

Trim Size is the final size of the book after it is printed and cut to be distributed. A 6x9 book will be 6 inches wide and 9 inches tall. As my first book was a book of poetry, I opted for the classic 6x9 trim size. However if you are writing a 450 page fiction novel, maybe you will go with the more traditional compact size often referred to as a "mass market paperback" (which Createspace, unfortunately, does not offer). If you want to sell your book in stores or on certain online retail sites, you must choose a standard industry size listed and the book must be between 24 and 858 pages long.

Different trim and different length (page count) sizes will result in different manufacturing (printing) costs. Books between 24 and 108 pages cost $2.15 per book (as a 6x9 as of 2016) and go up a few cents per few pages no matter what trim size you've selected. You may play around and experiment with what size book vs. what cost per book you are wanting. Obviously a 50 page book will cost less than a 500 page book to print. You can project your cost per book to print if you know approximately how many pages your book is and what trim size you want. Remember, your profit will be your list price minus the cost of printing, s&h, and royalty costs.

Additionally, the right text size will impact your page count. To choose the right text size, I simply picked a few books and counted how many characters (letters, numerals, spaces and punctuation marks) were in a line, which came to 60. Then I counted how many lines on a full page (which was roughly 30 to 40 lines depending on the book, some poetry books were 30 to 34 lines and some novels had more) and mirrored that to the document on my computer.

Custom trim sizes will only be sold on Amazon.com and your own personal Createspace e-store. You may select a template to download and use from the Interior options page or you can manually change the size of your document to match the Trim Size of your book.

To manually change it like I did, first decide your final Trim Size, open your book document (I use Microsoft Works Word Publisher) and go to:

"File"
"Page Setup"
"Source, Size, and Orientation"

Then select your custom size or change the width and height of your document to match the Trim Size selected for your published book. You can also change the size of the margins (the space between the text and the edge of the page) for the book in Page Setup.

Most professional books have a title page, a copyright page, a table of contents, a dedication, page numbers, an acknowledgements section, and an author bio. Some books even have the Book Title and Author Name on the tops of the left and right pages (respectively). Again, refer to your favorite books for comparison and see how they did it. (Author and book names can be added to each page in the Header options of your word processor.)

The Back Cover should include barcode, ISBN, list price and any taglines, descriptions, blurbs, or author info (and author pic). I, personally, chose to put the web address of my poetry site and the web address for my graphic design Facebook page on the back cover as well as on the last page of the book.

Books must have more than 100 pages in order to have spine text.

If the back cover design does not include a barcode, Createspace will include one in the lower left hand corner approximately .25" above the bottom trim line and .25" to the left of the spine. If you decide to use your own it must be 2" wide and 1.2" tall and must contain the 13 digit ISBN. I recommend leaving space on the back cover design and let Createspace issue and place the barcode.

Createspace will let you view all parts of the book, front and rear covers, and all internal pages before printing, so you may always make changes before final submission. Createspace does not put your list price on the barcode. You should put it elsewhere on the rear cover.

Createspace insists that it is not listed as the publisher in the book, online, or on any marketing or associated materials. The publisher assumes liability for the content and as such Createspace can only be listed as the Printer (if the author so wishes). Ultimately, the publisher is the one that gives the go ahead to print, make available to the public, and distribute the book.

When you have finished typing up your book, you can upload your work as a print-ready **.pdf**, **.doc**, **.docx**, or **.rtf** file. I used Microsoft Word and simply saved it as a rich text file (.rtf).

To do this, simply click

"File"
"Save As"
"Save as type"

"Rich Text File"

After you've uploaded your book, Createspace will do a page count and automatically check for any issues that need to be resolved before printing.

Near the bottom of the Interior page there is a link listed as **PDF Submission Guidelines**. If you click this, it will take you to a page with more specific information on trims, bleeds, live elements, blank pages, upside-down or overlapping text etc. There is also a link to download a free **CreateSpace Submission Specification** document under **Section 3: Checklist: Prepare for Printing** for further information. You can also download free templates for various Trim Sizes here.

After you upload your document, you will be able to view it in CreateSpace's **Interior Reviewer** where you can see your book page for page how it will look in a physical copy. Examine each page closely and carefully.

Images
Images may be CMYK or RGB color. All images should be sized at 100%, flattened to one layer and placed in your document at a minimum resolution of 300 DPI (dots per inch).

Cover

A great cover absolutely matters! If you are in a book store looking at a table of 25 books or so, you are going to pick up the one that sticks out the most. A great image and title should be attention grabbers! I used Self Pub Book Covers to choose my book cover. I would've had my book published 6 to 12 months earlier if I had had a reliable artist or designer return my inquiries. I spent months in wait. Finally, one day, I did a Google search for "pre-designed book covers" which resulted in a few sites that offered exactly that:

www.selfpubbookcovers.com
www.authormarketingclub.com
www.thebookcoverdesigner.com

Self Pub Book Covers offers over 9,000 unique designs and I found one that I fell in love with for $69. It was quite different than what I'd wanted at first but I felt it stood out so much more from similar covers (while also carrying the theme of my book) that I decided to snatch it up because once it's sold, it can never be resold to anyone else again. They use stock images to create unique book covers for sale. This means several of the elements of each book could be recycled for use in another book cover, but once you purchase the rights to the cover, they will never sell that exact cover again. It's better than it sounds. Check them out.

In the agreement, you agree to inform them once your book sells 250,000 copies which after that you must pay another one time extended license fee for under $100. Not too bad in my mind. Rich people problems, right?

After you find the right cover, you put your book title, subtitle (if you have one) and author name on the cover and choose the font, color, size, and place for each. They let you design and save your book covers in an online portfolio before purchase and offer unlimited edits afterward.

Other sites, you have to email the designer the book title and author name and they will place it for you and email you a copy back after you purchase the cover. I like Self Pub Book Covers because it's more design control in your hands. You can see it upfront and don't have to wait on anyone else. They give you a 72 DPI (for online use) and a 300 DPI image to use as the uploaded file for your book on CreateSpace. Plus unlimited text revisions, heck yes, right?

If you really don't want to splurge on a cover, check out www.fiverr.com (which I used for the cover of this book and only cost me $21). I've seen graphic designers offer book cover designs starting at $5. You can even design a book cover for free on CreateSpace if you already have an image that you would like to use. Make sure you own the rights to that image or Google search "free stock images of…." and whatever you're looking for. Createspace offers 30 different layout and design options for your cover with color, font, and stock image options.

There's nothing wrong with this option, however, I felt a more professional touch would really give my book a great polished look and I am extremely satisfied with how my cover from Self Pub Book Covers and Fiverr turned out. You can see it at www.AutumnShadows.webs.com or do a search on Amazon "Ryan Griffin Autumn Shadows".

If you REALLY don't want to spend any money at all on a cover, you can design it in **Microsoft Paint**, **GIMP** (a free version of Photoshop), **Microsoft Word** (there's a great step by step tutorial on www.thecreativepenn.com by author Joanna Penn in how to create your own cover in MS Word), www.canva.com, or www.befunky.com. Www.diybookcovers.com offers lots of free cover templates for personal use. Www.damonza.com is a pay cover design site however check out their portfolio if you just want some ideas on a great cover.

Check out the **Resources** section in the back of this book for sites that allow you to use stock photo images for free (no fees or royalties). Certain images can be used without attribution and others must be used with.

Creative Commons License means you can use an image in any way that you want even for commercial (to make money with) purposes. **Creative Commons with Attribution** means you can use an image in any way that you want as long as you site and credit the creator of the image.

After you've got your perfect cover, you can choose Matte or Glossy for it's surface finish. I chose glossy for my first book which is a poetry anthology. CreateSpace will design a cover for you starting at $399. This is the one place I actually used a professional and didn't simply do myself. I did everything else for my book; editing, formatting, table of contents, spacing, sizing, font, back cover design, author bio.

If you can't decide which version of a cover you like more, why not test it out and get feedback from strangers? Www.pickfu.com allows you to do just that for a small fee.

Fonts

Createspace can print lots of fonts. However, there are a few that Createspace does not recognize and will cause an issue to be found when using the **Interior Reviewer** application to proof your book. You must change fonts or embed them in your PDF. Embedding your fonts means that the font information travels with your document even to computers that do not have that font installed. You can download most fonts for free (even fonts used in famous movie or TV show titles). Just do a Google search for whatever font you are looking for and include the term "free download".

Uniformity

One thing that is extremely important that I overlooked with my first book is uniformity which means everything should be the same. All the chapter headings should be the same font, size, and style (bold, italics, etc). The one part I missed in the first printing of Autumn Shadows was that two of the quotes were italicized and so were the names behind it and two of the quotes were italicized but the names behind them were not. This is the smallest oversight to be had in printing a book but mattered to me as a perfectionist. I had it fixed (with a few other little typos) for the second printing.

So after your book is finished, go back and look at everything to make sure it matches, unless you do it differently on purpose. Make sure each chapter has the same amount of spaces from the top of the page to the chapter number or title, that the entire chapter heading text is uniform, same font size etc.

Fonts (not just the text size) will also change the length and page count of your book, choose one that fits what you are going for, just make sure it is readable. I recommend something like Times New Roman, Garamond, or Aparajita for main body text (all serif fonts: Serif simply meaning that the fonts tend to have sharp not blunt edges). Bebas Neue, Bank Gothic MD BT, Helvetica and Impact are some of my favorite fonts to use for headings or promotional material (flyers, business cards etc) and are simply sans-serif fonts (literally meaning "without" serif, or simply having blunted or rounded edges).

Different fonts create different tones (remember this for cover design). Again, I refer you to look at some of your favorite books to see what sort of font is used for the cover. Title and Author Name should contrast the background of the book.

After completing the **Title Information, ISBN, Interior,** and **Cover** sections, you may submit your final product to CreateSpace for approval. They are going to check the book to make sure it meets the technical aspects of the printer's requirements; they do not check spelling, grammar, accuracies for title or author info, or anything else. That is all on you.

They do, however, double check to make sure that the ISBN assigned to your book matches the one used in the book.

On the **Complete Setup** section, you may also download the link to the PDF Submission Guidelines or view the User Agreement (that contains the **Content Submissions** guide under section 2.3) here.

The Community section on CreateSpace is a great source for FAQs by fellow authors. If you have a specific question, most likely, someone else has already that question and already asked it there.

If you have a novel, and after it is finished, I recommend reading through it entirely to look for any spelling, grammatical, punctuation, continuity (of storyline), or other errors. Great authors are able to carry the mood and tone and resolve character arcs throughout the book too.

Realize that this is not an overnight process and that turning out a great product will require time, effort, extended attention, and attention to detail, towards it.

We, as readers, do not realize it but when we read familiar works, our brains automatically skip certain words; it is much harder to catch your own mistakes than for someone else to catch. My first book was a book of poetry, which, I forewent the expertise of an editor because most of it was simple and easy to catch the mistakes.

However, I did make revisions to poems and punctuation even after reading poems multiple times. If you have a great support system, have friends and family read your book with an eagle eye looking for all the mistakes that I pointed out above. When I finish writing my novels, I will probably hire the expertise of a professional editor.

A first time buyer of a book with many spelling or grammar mistakes will most likely not be a return customer if you continue to write and publish books. Remember, business is good, repeat business is better! Many famous authors only got there because they put out a great product and their readers continued to buy their other books. That is sometimes why a series (like Harry Potter) is a great success.

When you are finally ready to submit your book to Createspace for approval and to be sent to the printer, do so in the **Review** section. This will take up to 24 hours for them to review. I actually submitted Autumn Shadows five individual times, making little adjustments here and there, before finally being ready to receive my proof copy.

CreateSpace offers two proof options. I recommend the physical book format just because you get a real sense of how your book will look inside and out. You have to pay for printing cost and shipping and handling, but its negligible compared to the feeling of having your first printed copy in your hands.

I remember the extreme feeling of pride and accomplishment and how I treated it like gold when I received my proof copy. Exactly how it looks is exactly how the published copy will look. My proof copy didn't have page numbers, so I had to fix that and a few other little things (like punctuation) before being ready to publish and market to the world. I took a whole weekend to read through my book of poetry and make any little changes to it before deciding it was ready.

After you approve your proof copy online, you are now ready to publish and release it to the rest of the world.

Factoid:
The dot above a lowercase
'i' or 'j' is called a tittle.

7

FORMATTING

My proof copy of Autumn Shadows did not have page numbers. It was something I struggled to figure out and just forewent, figuring there was a slight chance Createspace might do it for me. They didn't.

They really print everything you submit as is. After looking over my proof copy, I decided it was necessary as every other book has page numbers and I can't very well have a Table of Contents with four different sections in my book without page numbers.

Page Numbers
To achieve this in Microsoft Word, you must go to **View**, then **Header and Footer**.

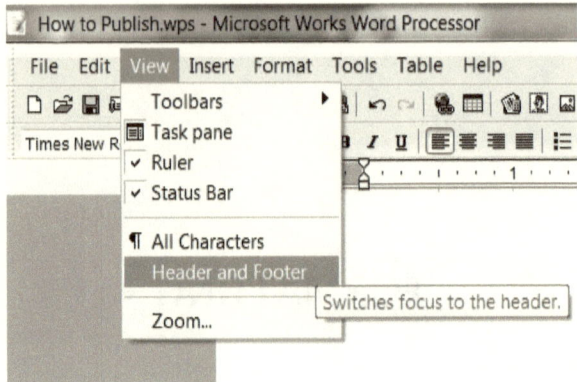

Then go back into your document, click on the Footer and go to **Insert** and select **Page Numbers**.

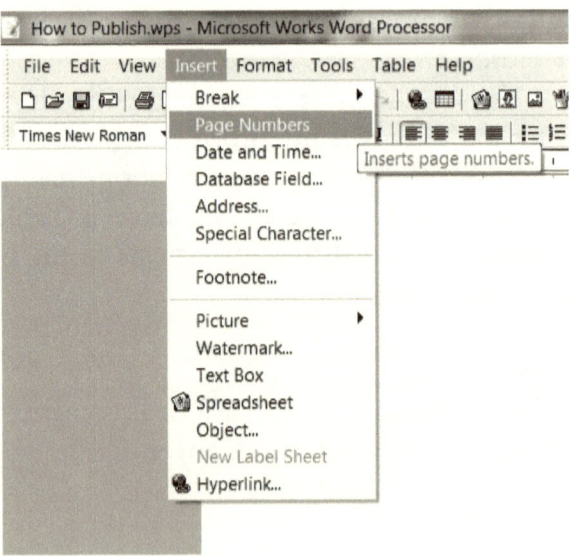

After you have your page numbers in place, you then have the option of deciding if you want it to start on the first or second page of your book and what page number to start with. I like to set my starting page to '1' and then select "No footer on first page". Do this in **File, Page Setup,** and **Other Options.**

If you add page numbers without using a header or footer, they will be part of the document text that will take up part of the line formatting allowing it to be moved or deleted. By using a footer, it ensures they are static and will not move as you edit your document.

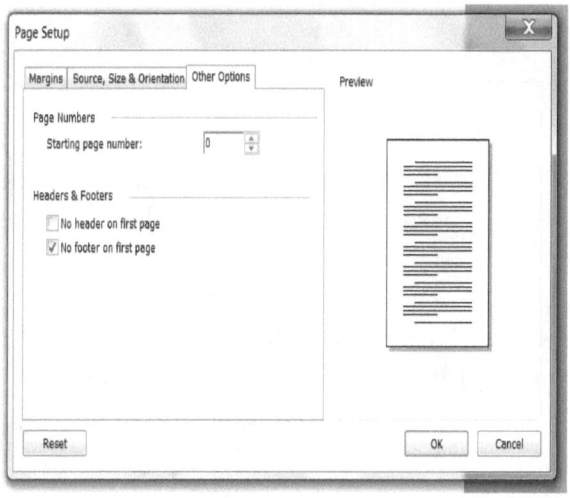

Alignment

Additionally, any book uses a type of alignment called **Justify** which is basically left and right at the same time. It takes an entire line of text and spaces it out evening so that the body of text evenly meets the margin on both sides. Simply put, it makes it look nicer but all professionals do it, so you should too. It's the 4th icon in your top menu in the alignment section.

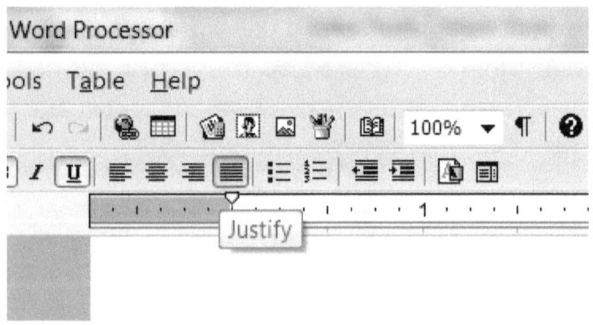

Now if for some reason your last line in the paragraph looks like this...

It's because you simply didn't press "Enter" after the paragraph, (doing so tells your document that you are starting a new paragraph).

Trim Sizes

Createspace offers 12 different industry standard

trim sizes to choose from ranging from 5x8 to 8x10. Different sizes will need to have different margins for printing. The longer the book, the bigger the margins should be. (Inside margin is the one by the crease/spine of the book, outside margins are the edge of the page opposite the crease and the top and bottom.) Createspace recommends at least .5" for all outside margins.

Page Count	Inside Margin	Outside Margins
24 to 150 pages	.375"	at least .25"
151 to 300 pages	.5"	at least .25"
301 to 500 pages	.625"	at least .25"
501 to 700 pages	.75"	at least .25"
701 to 828 pages	.875"	at least .25"

Factoid:
Publisher Bennet Cerf bet Dr. Seuss that he couldn't write a book using less than 50 different words. Dr. Seuss won that bet by writing Green Eggs and Ham.

8

DISTRIBUTION

Royalties to online retailers are calculated by a % of the list price plus a fixed charge plus a per page charge.

Scenario A
For a 184 page black and white book, you set your USD (U.S. Dollars) list price at $8.99. A customer purchases your book on Amazon.com and a book is printed to fulfill that order.

Sales Channel % = $3.60
Fixed Charge = $0.85
Per Page Charge total = $2.20
Your Royalty = $2.34

Scenario B
For a 184 page black and white book, you set your GBP's (Great British Pound) list price at 5.99 lbs. and your EUR (Euros) list price at 6.99.

A customer purchases your book on Amazon.co.uk via the Amazon Europe channel and a book is printed in continental Europe to fulfill that order.

Sales Channel % = 2.80
Fixed Charge = 0.60
Per Page Charge = 2.20
Your Royalty = 1.29 Euros.

Amazon's royalty rate is 40%
CreateSpace e-store is 20%
Expanded Distribution is 60%

In this section, you will choose where to make your book available, from online retailers like Amazon, Amazon Europe, and other expanded distribution channels to your very own CreateSpace e-store as well as book stores, colleges and libraries.

Under the **Description** section, you should write a brief yet concise description of your book. Maybe something like what would go on the back of your book to get people interested in reading it. Talk about the characters and major plots points without revealing anything to intimate. Feel free to compare it to other known titles or authors as well. This description will be displayed on your e-store and Amazon detail page.

Also, look at some of your favorite books (within the genre this book is). Most write in third person, present tense. Even though you are writing it, we'll pretend we are having a professional editor writing the book description and Author Biography. Just comes off much more professional this way. And remember, customers are fickle and emotional buyers; they can be swayed or turned off easily.

The Author Bio can help make or break the reader of what they think of you overall. Don't include your stance on politics or religion unless that's what the book is about. People are emotional creatures and can be turned off by someone of a completely different belief system even if they were interested in your book. Stick to your background as an author, any awards given, relevant groups or organizations you belong to, where your work may have been featured, how you relax in your downtime, what leisure activities you do, or a little something about your family or the area you live in. Again, read the author bios of some of your favorite authors. This helps readers connect with you on a deeper level.

The Author Bio should also be written in the third person. Any author believes in his own work or thinks he's interesting. It's a given. By writing in the third person, we convince our readers that other people think we're interesting too, enough to write a book description, blurb, or bio about us and that might be reason enough to interest your reader.

Next is your **BISAC** (Book Industry Standards and Communications) category. This makes it easier for retailers to categorize your book and for customers to find your book. If your cookbook is categorized as Sci-Fi, the right customer will never find it.

You can also select what language it is written (and printed in) and what the country of publication is. Different countries have different laws and tax codes.

The Search Keywords are important in helping your potential customer find your book online. Stick to keywords that have to do with genre, theme, and content.

Autumn Shadows keywords were something like: *Poetry, dark, poems, shadow, gothic.*

How to Publish for Next to Nothing's keywords are: *How, Publish, Guide, Book, Author.*

Anything someone might type in when looking for a book close to what you are offering.

You also have the option to select **Contains Adult Content** (if your book is sexually or violently graphic) and **Large Print** (lots of elderly or vision impaired customers like books in Large Print, so if that is your market or demographic, you may want to consider it.)

Factoid:
Suzanne Collins, author of the
Hunger Games, used to write for
Nickelodeon including the show
Clarissa Explains It All.

9

PRICING

Ideally, how much would you like to sell your book for? (Your answer). Great! Now forget that number! We are going to come up with the price for your book from the opposite end of the spectrum. Instead of thinking about how much you could sell your book for as an author, think along the lines of your consumer, your readers. If you were looking at your book (while trying to be as arbitrary as possible), what is the most you would pay for your book?

If you're not sure the amount or unsure if you're being completely unbiased, ask a handful of close friends or family members. Or even better, ask a complete group of strangers in a café or an online group. Since strangers are your target audience after friends and family members, some demographic research is never a bad thing.

All of your pricing and marketing

decisions should have the customer in mind and what better way to do that than to adopt the perspective of a prospective buyer?

It's okay to want to make some profit on your book, but that should not be the driving force behind setting the price. I would set it a few dollars below what you would find in a similar book in a store or online (as far as content, style, professional quality, book length etc).

When I first published, I wanted every dollar from every book that I could get. The more I read and learned about the industry though, the more I found how common it is to give away free books for marketing purposes.

Not only is a book a part of you, but it's a premium business card as well. A book with your name on it certainly makes you look like an expert or an authority on the subject or field. Hand it out to publishers and in contests as well. People lose and throw away business cards; no one throws a book away. I like the notion of offering free digital versions of previous books with the purchase/pre-purchase of a new book or as an incentive to signing up to an email list.

So when choosing a sell price, remember, you're an unknown first time author. See the price that your favorite author is selling his book? You're nowhere near his level of familiarity or fandom. I've read estimates that as many as

300,000 books are published every year, how many are similar to yours as far as content, style, and price? Realize this and know that you have to offer your potential reader an incentive to buy YOUR book instead of one just like it. A cheaper price definitely helps.

Also, if you take the route I did, you're a self published author. That means there is no guarantee of how well the writing, content, story, or editing is. People who buy from authors published by professional publishing companies are accustomed to a certain quality of product, so that's why the price is often higher with traditional publishers.

Remember, incentive! Don't worry about (just) profits in the beginning (other than losing money in the process) but focus on building a loyal fan base that will continue to buy your products, follow your career, and recommend your work to others.

How much would a book similar to yours (quality, content, size, & page count) cost in a book store?

Autumn Shadows most likely would be $11.99 in a book store if published by a major publisher (going off of quality of cover, back cover design, description, blurbs, copyright page, content, format, writing etc.) I really went the extra mile in making sure I had all the key elements there. I set the list price for Autumn Shadows at $7.99 after wrestling with the idea of $6.99 in the beginning because I knew it was about quantity of book sales as opposed to quantity of dollars per sale. I settled at $7.99 instead of $8.99, $9.99 or any higher price because I wanted to keep the price relatively low to entice any potential customers but also still make a little more profit than barely breaking even. So I had my price!

Friends and family even offered me $10 a book but I demanded they take their change, saying "the price is the price". I wasn't going to charge $10 to family and $8 to strangers. If anything, I wanted to do the opposite. I wish I could've offered them a better price but after all the money I'd spent on printing and shipping/handling; I needed to start making it back. Basically everyone, friend or stranger, got the friends and family discount.

I ordered 85 copies of my first book to give to friends and family (after having done an online survey of seeing who wanted one beforehand, which ended up being in the 30s). I ordered about 50 more figuring on book stores, signings, other events etc.

Some people bought a copy just because they knew me, not necessarily because they liked dark poetry, which was a nice gesture. They were essentially supporting a struggling author.

I've seen some self published books with outrageous prices. Someone published a book of poems for $12.99. On Amazon, you can see the page count of a book. So I'm thinking okay, maybe something close to mine, maybe a little more (mine was 148 pages). Nope. Not even 100 pages. Not even 75. Not even 50. The book was 33 pages long. This author must be the Picasso of poetry or Robert Frost's descendant or something to think a 33 page book of poems is worth $12.99. Maybe that's the price they'd like to get for it. But you have to market from the consumer's viewpoint. And of all the millions of books and all the thousands of books of poetry, why is someone going to pay $12.99 for a book only 33 pages long? Boggles my mind. I hope they are successful and become a best selling author but I just don't see it happening.

No matter what you do, author, poet, artist, rock star, the first business you are in is **Marketing**. What you sell is the second business you are in. Figure out your demographic, market to them, and sell from the buyer's viewpoint.

What factors determine your decision to buy a product? Price? Quality? Style? Positive Reviews? There are many things I look at when buying something online. Everything that you take into consideration a purchase, others do as well. As frugal or fickle as you are, there are people out there that are exponentially worse. And they have to find your book before deciding to buy or pass on it.

The average person has an attention span of 6 seconds. You have to hook them into wanting to learn more about your book (or product) in those 6 seconds. Then you have about 20 seconds to keep them interested while they wrestle around with the idea if it might be worth purchasing. After that you have three to four minutes to fully influence their decision to purchase while they look over all the details of the book.

We want to give the ones that do find your book, as much reason to buy your book as possible. That means quality of cover and content, no spelling or noticeable grammatical or punctuation mistakes. A smooth polished look and feel. Absolutely nailing all of the components of a professional well put together book and then the right price (which to the buyer, lower is always better, isn't it?).

There is a classic formula for writing and publishing a great book (or any product) and successfully marketing it. Some are able to do it without putting in as much effort, but we want to give you (the author) as much chance as we can by offering the consumer as much as we can.

In order to maximize profits for my first book while keeping the price low, I configured the costs of printing along with shipping and handling costs so that I could see exactly how much profit each book would yield. Below is table for Createspace with s&h charges built into the price and redistributed evenly per book. Also keep in mind the printing costs for Autumn Shadows (a 6x9 book with 148 pages @ $2.62 per book with sale price of $7.99).

# of books+s&h cost=cost per copy=profit per book

1) + $3.59 s&h = 6.21 cost per copy = $1.78 profit
2) + $4.18 s&h = 4.71 cost per copy = $3.28 profit
3) + $4.77 s&h = 4.21 cost per copy = $3.78 profit
4) + $5.36 s&h = 3.96 cost per copy = $4.03 profit
5) + $5.95 s&h = 3.81 cost per copy = $4.18 profit
6) + $6.54 s&h = 3.71 cost per copy = $4.28 profit
7) + $7.13 s&h = 3.64 cost per copy = $4.35 profit
8) + $7.72 s&h = 3.59 cost per copy = $4.40 profit
9) + $8.31 s&h = 3.54 cost per copy = $4.45 profit
10) + $8.00 s&h = 3.42 cost per copy = $4.57 profit
11) + $8.50 s&h = 3.39 cost per copy = $4.60 profit
12) + $9.00 s&h = 3.37 cost per copy = $4.62 profit
13) + $9.50 s&h = 3.35 cost per copy = $4.64 profit
14) + $10.00 s&h = 3.33 cost per copy = $4.66 profit
15) + $10.50 s&h = 3.32 cost per copy = $4.67 profit

16) + $11.00 s&h = 3.31 cost per copy = $4.68 profit
17) + $11.50 s&h = 3.30 cost per copy = $4.69 profit
18) + $12.00 s&h = 3.29 cost per copy = $4.70 profit
19) + $12.50 s&h = 3.28 cost per copy = $4.71 profit
20) + $13.00 s&h = 3.27 cost per copy = $4.72 profit
25) + $15.50 s&h = 3.24 cost per copy = $4.75 profit
30) + $18.00 s&h = 3.22 cost per copy = $4.77 profit
35) + $20.50 s&h = 3.21 cost per copy = $4.78 profit
40) + $23.00 s&h = 3.08 cost per copy = $4.91 profit
45) + $25.50 s&h = 3.19 cost per copy = $4.80 profit
50) + $23.00 s&h = 3.08 cost per copy = $4.91 profit
55) + $25.00 s&h = 3.07 cost per copy = $4.92 profit
60) + $27.00 s&h = 3.07 cost per copy = $4.93 profit
65) + $29.00 s&h = 3.06 cost per copy = $4.93 profit
70) + $31.00 s&h = 3.06 cost per copy = $4.93 profit
75) + $33.00 s&h = 3.06 cost per copy = $4.93 profit
80) + $35.00 s&h = 3.06 cost per copy = $4.93 profit
85) + $37.50 s&h = 3.05 cost per copy = $4.94 profit
90) + $39.00 s&h = 3.05 cost per copy = $4.94 profit
95) + $41.00 s&h = 3.05 cost per copy = $4.94 profit
100) + $43.00 s&h = 3.05 cost per copy = $4.94 profit

As you can see from this order guide, the profit from ordering two books instead of one almost doubles. Ideally we want to order as many as we think we are going to logically be able to sell plus a few dozen more in order to maximize profits. To do this, we don't just want to ask our friends and family if they'd be interested, we want to directly ask them "Who IS going to buy a book when they are ready?" It draws more of a solid response.

The reason to order physical copies to sell instead of allowing everyone to buy online is that they can get it signed and save on s&h by getting it from me (as I still sold it at list price) and I got more of a profit than I would if they bought it online (through Amazon or my own e-store).

When you order and sell books through yourself, there is no middle man and no one to give royalties to. Incentive for you and the buyer, a definite win/win.

In the order guide, there was a shipping and handling price break right around the 50 book mark. It's possible that they give a small discount for bulk shipping, (this is merely my suspicions, but is unconfirmed as the actual reason). I urge you to check for yourself after your book is ready and do the math yourself.

As you can see, the profit jump starts to slow down drastically after book 5 and then to just one penny after book 14 until it starts to repeat in the 90's.

Like I said earlier, I ordered 85 books because I had roughly 35 people say they would buy a book and I wanted enough to be able to do book signings and for everyone who would want one but didn't reserve a copy. 85 is a lot when you're paying for it up front but I saw it as a great investment and I did make a decent profit per copy sold. After two months, I had about 20 books left, had given away maybe ten to family, a few as Christmas presents, and one in an online contest giveaway. If I'd have sold all 85 copies, I would've made a profit of $419.90. So the upfront costs are completely justified if you can sell more than what it costs to print and ship the books.

I also suggest donating a few books to local libraries and charities or fundraiser events to help support your community and to get your name out there. This helps in two ways (while you don't make money directly from donating) you 1) expose yourself as an author and 2) gain attention to new people that may not have found you otherwise and become tied to a good cause, which might make someone more likely to pick up your book or buy a copy if the profits go towards a charity (to them it's killing two birds with one stone because they get a book they wanted but might not have wanted to spend money on but do it because the money goes toward a charity or good cause).

I did a book signing with a few other local authors and they sold their novels/novellas for $5 a piece. I think the one was 80 pages and the other was 200 pages or so. So I don't think they made much at all. There's nothing wrong with this approach if you only write because you want your audience to read your work. The typical writer will write (usually) for one of three reasons.

- So others read their work
- To make money
- To be famous

Instead of opting for only one, I am probably all three parts equally and would want to achieve success with all three proportionately. Each writer must define success for themselves however and strategize accordingly.

Additionally, because we are selling books, we are required to report our earnings and pay the proper amount of tax. CreateSpace will issue you a 1099MISC form with your total royalties paid in the prior tax year.

Factoid:
The oxford comma is included after the second to last item in a list (before the word 'and') such as: eggs, bacon, bread, and Ben and Jerry's. It would not be used after the noun "Ben" because Ben is part of the proper noun "Ben and Jerry's".

10

MARKETING & PROMOTION

I'm published! Now what? Now that your book is ready for purchase, the next step is to market it! Your job as a writer stops when the book is completed, however your job in marketing your book never stops. Until your name is associated with multiple best sellers, your books actually never just fly off the shelves by themselves. You must market and put them in front of people to view.

My first piece of advice is to find websites, Facebook pages, and groups dedicated to authors, writers, and publishing, as many as you can. Find and join, like, or bookmark them. Join email lists and subscribe to marketing coaches and bloggers.

Soak up as much information as you can get, read all of the frequently asked questions, ask your own, and learn as much about the process as you can as you are bound to learn many things that I will not cover here. This will be a basic introduction into the world of marketing and promoting your book as I am still relatively new to it myself.

I have subscribed to some email lists that I later took myself off of just because the information was very generic or not very relevant, but you won't find the great ones unless you cast a wide net. **Mandy Wallace** and **JF Penn (The Creative Penn)** are some of my favorite coaches to follow. **The Write Life** and **Writer's Circle** sites are great to follow too. Why? They deliver lots of great content!

By joining lots of pages or groups and networking with others in writing and publishing, not only can you learn from them but you can be exposed to other sources of great information.

Consider joining other writing groups or book clubs as well. And just realize that like any other craft, it really does take years to become expert at or an authority on any subject.

I looked for a Facebook author group for the area I lived in and didn't find what I was looking for so I created the **Central PA Local Author Network**. I designated this group for authors and aspiring authors to share tips and tricks and network with one another. I wanted to know where other authors were doing book signings, what events they were participating in, and what book stores they had their books in and wanted to share what I knew as well. In a way, while new authors are learning the ropes of the business, we also get to teach and mentor aspiring authors in the process.

Some great places to market and sell your books are poetry/fiction groups (www.meetup.com), local small individually owned book stores. I've had way more success with small stores than I have with big chains. Small stores offer a better return on the sale of the book as well. Most chain book stores want 50 percent of the sell price.

Some stores have purchased books from me and some have asked to do consignment which means they pay me no money until they sell the book. Generally starting out, (since beggars can't be choosers), I will ask for and offer a certain percentage to the store and to me, but will generally accept whatever terms the store wants to do since exposure is so important when starting out. If a store wants 50% and I want 70% ROI (Return On Investment), I'm still going to negotiate but will accept whatever we land at (unless they ask for something ridiculous like 70% or more, that won't even cover costs, I'd actually lose money). And I'd accept up to 50% because 50% of *something* is better than 70% of *nothing.*

Individually owned book stores will offer 60/40 or relatively close to that. I got to keep all of the profits from a craft show book signing and a small book store signing because I created a flyer to help promote the event. The owners were grateful for the extra promotion and I was grateful for the extra profits.

Social Media

There are worlds of social media and sale sites to become a part of. There's Facebook, Twitter, Instagram, Youtube, Goodreads, Pinterest, all great for connecting with readers or other authors. (Youtube? For books? Really? Yes!) Lots of authors create trailers for their books just like movies do.

It's hard to maintain a presence on all of them, so I suggest picking two to three that you want to create a strong and interactive presence on instead of having a dozen accounts that you barely use.

Remember, part of marketing is creating a tribe of passionate fans, this means answering questions, helping others with what you know about the industry, promoting, asking questions about your readers, anything to connect with your fans. This is how you grow a strong following.

An author I recently met said that if you're

only selling books to friends and family, then you need to go make some new friends. Do this by interacting and connecting with readers (and writers!) online. Definitely one of the best pieces of advice I've heard so far.

Create an Amazon author page. Createspace is a partner of Amazon and when you publish through them, selling on Amazon will be one of your biggest markets. You can do so here: www.authorcentral.amazon.com.

Create a Gravatar (internet speak for Globally Recognized Avatar). It's an avatar of yourself as an author that works in conjunction with many social media sites including Wordpress blogs. Check out www.gravatar.com.

Go onto www.linkedin.com and Google Plus and list your occupation as writer or author. If you don't market yourself as a writer, no one else is going to accept you as a writer. If you write, you're a writer. As soon as you publish a work, you're an author. Own the title! And if you don't really feel like a writer yet, fake it until you make it.

The business world, just like most areas of life, are virtually unknown territories, most of us have to feel our way through them until we get a grasp for how it works. Guess what, you're not the only one who doesn't have it all figured out yet. Don't be afraid to show confidence in yourself though. One thing the Marine Corps taught me is that confidence (in yourself) breeds confidence (from others).

Becoming an Expert

They say everyone has a book stuck in them although maybe not everyone is meant to be a career author. Doesn't mean that everyone can't still write and publish a book. I've found that the older I get, the more I like to learn and the more I like to share and to teach what I've learned. In a way, by following this model, you become an expert on your subject matter (if you know enough about it). Consultants are paid big fees. Study everything you can about what it is that you love and then why not possibly write a book about it?

Applying to and becoming part of recognized institutions and organizations lends credibility to you as an expert as well, even though most likely that person is just like you or I but filled out some paperwork and got their name listed somewhere.

Not too far into my newfound career as an author, I'd soon started to realize too that the more I learned, the more I had the desire to share what I knew with other aspiring authors to help them fulfill their dreams. And the more I learned and the more I helped others, the more I started to become an expert or authority in the field of writing and publishing.

Having great knowledge and a desire to share it with the world, no matter what field you're in, can lead to speaking gigs, being a featured guest and others pointing their friends and family to you when they need help in that field.

My love of writing and love of teaching has also led me to put my skills to use in the workplace. I've worked in probably at least four different occupational fields over the last twelve years and for my last two positions, I wrote training manuals for both of them. One was a 22 page manual that covered six different stations for one of the biggest pizza chains in the country; the other was a 44 page guide for a small franchise mostly populating the northeast.

The fact that I wrote these did a few things, it created a central basis for training and knowledge for all employees and it absolutely looks great on a resume. You could literally write the book on how to do your job and in doing so, become the originator of most of the workplace knowledge and set yourself apart from your peers. It also creates an upper edge against other candidates applying for the same position that you are applying for.

Promotional Material

I discovered www.webs.com through some online ad on Facebook or similar site and had wanted a site to compile and display all of my poetry onto. It was fully customizable and I reeled at the potential to create a site from scratch. I picked a free theme that they offered and customized it with my own logo, banner, font, subpages, and music that played automatically when you view the site.

I spent dozens of man-hours working it until it was complete. I studied online guides and tutorials for basic HTML lessons and learned (through trial and error) how to create a website. I uploaded text, pictures, links, and videos and discovered it really was not that hard to do at all. I even created and designed two additional websites, one for a local annual charity fundraiser that I am a part of and one for my daughter's preschool because they did not have one. I designed and maintained it for a deduction of her enrollment costs in the pre-school. The teachers and parents loved it (and I learned how to do it all for free).

A personal site used for your writing is one of the bigger components of properly marketing yourself. I also designed custom business cards to hand out to readers, book stores, libraries, etc.

I created a book trailer using **Windows Live Movie Maker (**Apple users should have the **iMovie** app on their Macs). I uploaded pictures depicting several poems in my book, added some text to each frame, uploaded some music that fit the theme, and a few video segments to use as well. Movies have trailers, so why not books as well? One customer told me directly they bought Autumn Shadows just because of the trailer.

A good website should also have a calendar of events (for signings and appearances etc), an e-store where people can actually buy your book, an author bio (just like your book has), a blog where you regularly post good quality content on writing, publishing, or your experience as a writer (or whatever it is that you write about i.e. cooking, engineering etc.), and a way to sign up for emails (or to be a site member).

Webs.com lets me send out email blasts to all of my members should I want to.

You should also have a Facebook page because Facebook is the biggest social media giant right now. Use as many social media sites as you want to be active on. Engage other writers and readers in discussion, answer questions, gain an online presence in your circles and become the go to person or authority in whatever your field is.

Once you have people's ear, you can refer

them to your book or if they begin to research you, they can find it on your social media profiles.

As an author, you need to have a lot more at your table than just your books. Consider purchasing these things to help you market yourself as a legitimate author, not that you aren't but the public must see you this way.

- **Bookstands** to show off your books

- **Business cards** (and a **holder**) for your book or website with an email address and only a business phone number if you don't mind calls from strangers. (I'd rather get emails from strangers which I can just as easily give them my phone number afterwards if I would want to.)

- **Bookmarks or postcards**. If you do make some, put a brief description of your book on it, your most popular blurb, where it's available, links to websites, an email address and an author pic as well as the cover of your book. Same should go on a bookmark. To be honest, I don't really get the Author Postcard thing, but some authors love them. To me, postcards are too big to be practical, I feel like they are just going to sit in a drawer somewhere. I like bookmarks and business cards a lot better for freebies.

- **Tablecloth** - Pick any color you want, but definitely add it to your author bug-out bag. It makes a table at an event look so much more professional. Most in door events will provide you with a table and chair (although it's always good to make sure first before showing up with just books. Can you imagine doing a signing without a table? You wouldn't think it could happen but I've heard some pretty funny stories from other authors. Always best to check ahead of time.)

- **Stand up sign** - I use a 4x6 acrylic stand up sign with an author bio in it that talks about my style, genre, and book. Pretty much what you'd read in the About the Author section in the back of a book.

- **Bowl of candy** - This is completely optional but I think it's a great way to attract people. I usually have a bowl of Dove chocolate, Hershey kisses or mints for each of my signings. People love freebies, give them a reason to stop by the table and linger.

- **Pens and more pens!** - Always have a small cache of pens with you for an event. Not only will other authors at your event forget to bring them will want to share yours if you are at the same table but customers will lackadaisically walk off with them too. It's annoying, but I'd rather bring spares that way I'm never without one when needed. And remember, you're living your dream, don't sweat the small stuff.

- **Beverage(s)** I'll usually bring a 16 oz bottle of water if it's 2 hours or under and I'll bring a cooler with ice and water/soda if it's an all day event especially one where you have to speak to an audience or do an author panel Q&A.

- **Banners/posters (and easel)** - These are awesome things to attract more people to your table and make you stand out however they are not always practical. I've done events where I'm crammed into a small space with 8 or 10 other authors and there would be just no where to hang a banner or put up an easel and poster and I've done events where it's just one or two other authors and there's lots of room. Those are the optimal types of situations you would want to break out your big items for.

- **Small bills to make change!** - If you're selling the books yourself, you need to be able to make change for 10s and 20s. I usually bring $50 in ones and $50 in fives. Because I tend to have a propensity to over prepare for most situations, I was able to make change for a $100 bill at a street fair. I know your first thought is who brings a $100 bill to street fair but that was all she had and because I had a few $10s and $20s in my pocket, I was able to make change and capture that sale. I carry about $100 total between ones and fives when I expect to sell up to 20 books. If you plan on selling more, prepare a larger cash amount beforehand.

- **Credit Card Reader** - Truly legit merchants won't just accept cash but credit cards also. You can get a free Credit Card Reader (that plugs into your phone or tablet) from www.paypal.com with a free business account or from www.squareup.com. There's no monthly fees involved for either but each instead takes a small percentage off of each transaction. 2.7% for Paypal, 2.75% for Square. Remember these small fees are better than not making a sale at all because a potential buy may have run out of cash.

- **Canopy** - I recently did a street fair with two other local authors and I'd never sold books at an outside event before so I really didn't know what to expect. However, in addition to bringing a table and chairs, we set up a canopy to give us some shade and we were so glad that we did because it was 100° F that day. I spent all my time under the canopy and still wound up sunburned somehow. So a canopy really helped control how hot we were by giving some shade to us and to everyone that stopped by our table.

- **Sunscreen** - If it's an outside event, you're going to want it.

Making the Sale

As a new author, I've had the privilege of doing book signings in several stores in my area with other local authors and even a few big names (at least in the horror genre). I've also done a street fair where I've sold way more books than I have at any book store. It's weird but it's awesome too. I'm very open to non conventional events and venues than just book stores or book oriented events. The street fair was nice because there was no other competition as far as what we were offering. My two fellow local authors and I shared a table (and we all had different genres which was nice). Basically, we cornered the market at that venue.

At first, it was slow. We casually yelled out things like "Local authors here!" and other generic things. Because all three of us have a strong sense of humor, we started to say things like "Local authors, you don't have to read 'em, you just have to buy 'em!" and "If I sell all these books, my girlfriend will let me come home tonight!" It captured a lot of smiles and a few laughs. It was a good ice breaker. Then we decided to engage passers-by with questions like "Hey guys, what do you like to read?" or "What kind of books are you into?" That simple engagement stopped a lot of people and they walked over to our table just to talk with us. We weren't beings "sales-y".

Nobody wants to be sold anything. As a matter of fact, I don't try to sell anyone, I just try to introduce them to my book and let the book sell itself with its content, style, cover design etc. However you can't put a book into someone's hand if you can't even get their attention or get them to stop at your table. So how do you actually accomplish this?

The trick is to not jump right to the sale. With the rise of social media sites, the internet, video games, streaming music, movies etc, attention spans are at an all time low. I've read that the average internet surfer has an attention span of six seconds. Just six seconds skimming something before deciding to move on or learn more about it.

Step number one is to just catch their eye (if they're surfing a site) or their ear if they're walking by. You do this by having something relevant or interesting to them. In person, humor is a great way to break the ice. Many people start speeches with a joke to put everyone in a light mood. However online, you don't have that option, your cover is the first thing they are going to notice about your book, so if it doesn't pop or look professionally polished, you aren't going to keep their interest and then you've lost them forever. And let's face it, we're all told not to judge a book by its cover but we all do it anyway. People like to use logic and reason with everything that they do, especially purchases, but many times emotion plays a big part in it too.

Step two happens once you've captured their attention. Once you've made it past that initial six second timeframe, you have about 20 seconds to keep them interested in learning more about your product or book. We aren't trying to make a sale yet; we are trying to show them the value in whatever you're offering. If they like everything about it and you've kept their attention for that 20 second timeframe, then you move into the decision making timeframe. This lasts usually two to six minutes as the customer weighs all of the factors into purchasing your book (or product). They are going to look at reviews, blurbs, the price, and any incentives you are offering.

Incentives like freebies help motivate purchases. Think about offering a free e-download of a previous book if they preorder your new one. I donated all of the profits of Autumn Shadows sold over the course of about six weeks to the PA Veterans Foundation in the six weeks prior to a fund raising event I take part of every year.

People love a good cause and even though I didn't make any money off of the books during those six weeks, it put my book in the hands of a lot of readers and even if we can't make money off of that individual book, we are planting the seed of a return customer if they like what they read.

And that's the goal. Because while business is good, repeat business is better. I don't just want someone to buy my book. I want someone to buy all of the future books I put out as well.

Writing a series is a great way to get readers hooked and keep them coming back for future sequels (purchases).

So to recap, the sales process looks like this:

- Capture their attention
- Keep them interested in learning about the book
- Incentivize them by offering them additional value
- Finally, convert a prospect into a sale

Prospects can and will leave the sales process at any given time for any reason, so reduce those chances by optimizing every aspect of the book and the mindset of the customer by implementing controls to combat the factors that would lose someone's attention and the sale.

Offer an incentive when launching a book like 25% off of your next book just for leaving a review in the first 48 hours. Or a free copy of your current book to anyone that left you a review of your last book.

Promotions and giveaways are big draws for gaining email addresses and getting loyal followers. There are 3 different types of promotions.

A sweepstake is a random giveaway which basically says a winner of a book or other prize will be randomly selected from a group. You may not ask for special considerations like following you or liking your Facebook page and certainly not for any cash contribution or donation.

A contest measures some sort of skill and you may charge a reasonable fee for this. However there is to be no luck in a contest even in the event of a tie. Introducing an element of luck converts the contest into an illegal lottery.

A lottery is a random drawing that charges a fee. This is illegal in all 50 states (without proper permits) and is punishable under law. Avoid these types of promotions.

If you are doing a book signing and aren't getting much attention at your table, don't just sit there, get up and interact with other customers, ask them what they like to read. If they don't read what you write, just talk to them about books that they like. If you strike up a conversation, you can slip in that you write books and you can show it to them. If you were pleasant and cordial, they may get it for someone else.

I'll be looking for other street fairs and unconventional venues where local authors can get some exposure and make some sales. Don't limit yourself to traditional venues. Contact local coffee shops, groups, organizations, libraries etc about selling your book (and giving them a portion). After "How to Publish for Next to Nothing" is published, I plan on going around to local businesses to see if they'd be interested in featuring and selling my book in their store.

I also have my first Book Expo scheduled in a few months where I'll have a table along with about 100 other authors. I'm sure it will draw in a big crowd, but I'll be competing for the attention of potential customers with about 100 others as well. I'm not going to try to market my book (make a sale) to everyone that passes by. My goal is to find the customers interested in the genre of books I am selling and strike up a conversation with them.

Blogging is a great way to stay relevant and in the forefront of a potential buyer's mind. I hate filler and emails that waste my time, don't offer me any incentive or information about the craft of writing or publishing and jump right to the sale. All of these things turn me off as a potential buyer.

My business strategy will look something like this: blog regularly about things that I enjoy writing about and genuinely have an interest in. Be knowledgeable and share the information, tips & tricks, and tools of the trade that I come across. Offer an email subscription service that will have links to my blog in it and the things I just mentioned that I know other writers will find value in. Always have my books available to all of my readers whether through links in the email or at the end of the blog or whatever.

They should always be able to trace their way to your e-store or Amazon page or wherever you prefer to sell your books. You don't have to try to sell everyone every time with every email but the info should be readily available.

I'll also send out the occasional email talking about any new books or projects I'm working on to keep the fans updated but I'll capture email subscribers by offering good actionable content that they can use or learn from and never filler. I know this is what I look for in the gurus and online coaches I follow, so that's what I'll offer.

Create a Tribe

Something I am going to be working on next as I approach the publication of this book is starting a loyal following and email subscription list. There are a million lists to belong to, why should someone subscribe to yours? Two reasons: Good content and incentive!

I hate getting emails just for the sake of getting emails. I followed so many coaches and signed up for so many lists that many of them were just sending daily emails talking about nothing or their day to day activities that somehow tied into being a writer. Like their strategy was simply to bombard people with their presence until they finally gave into purchasing their coaching package. My time was too valuable for that; it was valuable content (about writing or publishing) that I sought after.

I soon began to purge my email subscriptions until I had only a handful of really good coaches and bloggers sending me quality content (usually once or twice a month, perfect, not overloading my inbox).

I've mentioned good/quality content a few times now. So what exactly do I mean? I'm talking about knowledge and information that your reader can apply to their craft or book. I don't care that you like to eat scrambled eggs in the morning before you write. Did you really just send me an email to tell me about that? Unsubscribed.

Remember, knowledge isn't power. Applicable knowledge is power. There's lots of useless info out there. As a growing writer, I want good quality content, so that's the only thing you should be sending to your subscribers outside of the occasional email talking about your book signing or book launch release.

While you grow your tribe, you should offer a few loyal readers or friends an incentive to promote you or your book. Send them a free copy of your book or mention them in the book's acknowledgments. Get them to mention you in any relevant conversations, advertise for you by word of mouth, online or in person, and post honest reviews online. People trust their friends more than a stranger trying to sell them something.

Amazon #1 Bestseller Lists

Amazon has two best seller lists for every category: Paid and Free. You want to maximize your book launch every way you can and one of the best ways to do that is to offer it for free on Amazon (the higher it is on the bestseller list, the more people will see it).

While giving your book away for free won't yield you any immediate income, it will create followers and give you exposure to the literary world. Set yourself up for success by taking advantage of Amazon's five days of free downloads every 90 days.

It takes time and investment to create a following. One of the best ways to attract new customers (readers) is a free give-away. Create an incentive for them to sign up to an email subscription list like a free download or audio version of your book.

One of the things I always look for when considering subscribing to someone is good content, no filler. Don't send me an email just to send it. I hate being flooded and spammed with emails that don't offer or barely offer any good content for me as a reader or writer. I'm looking for tips and advice on how to become a better writer, how to better market myself, how to attract more readers/customers, and how to make my book better.

If you send me regular emails that don't talk about these things, I usually unsubscribe and as I try to think about my writing from a customer's perspective, this is the type of material I plan on offering to my subscribers, no filler, just great content.

Once you do set up an email subscription list, there are certain federal laws you must comply with.

Spam laws provide that a sender must meet certain criteria before mass distribution emails be sent out.

- Must get the recipient's permission to email them. This means not emailed everyone in your online address book and automatically subscribing them. That is illegal.
- Subject line must be relevant to the text contained therein
- Must contain an unsubscribe or opt-out button or link
- Must not contain unsolicited marketing or pornographic material
- Must have friendly from email address (not

one that is sent from then immediately deleted)

- Must not use harvested email addresses (basically email addresses that are stolen, borrowed, or purchased without the email owners knowledge and permission).

There are some exceptions and continuations but these are the basic guidelines. Just get the email owners permission to send them email, keep the emails relevant to what they agreed to be emailed about, and offer an unsubscribe feature and you should be fine.

The FTC can fine you if you do not comply with spam laws especially with the opt-out feature. It's considered harassment after that.

Additionally once you obtain their email addresses, sometimes you will obtain personal information too (name, age, location etc). You need to make sure it is protected and not shared and let them know what you do with and how you protect any information gathered.

Any private information that is gathered via email or on by website membership needs to be addressed. You must put a privacy policy statement at the bottom of your site. If you do not share information with other parties, say so. If you do, make sure it is not personally identifiable to members (usually statistical purposes only are shared i.e. pages visited, time spent on pages etc).

Children 13 and under are further protected by laws like COPPA (Children's Online Privacy Protection Act) which requires a parent's permission to use certain sites and features.

Most social media websites do not allow users 13 and under to create accounts because of how difficult it is to comply with these types of laws.

Author Website

Every modern author must have a website to market themselves with. It is an absolute must. There are lots of sites out there that offer free websites that you can create and customize to fit your style and brand. It can be a tad daunting but it's really not that bad.

I've had no formal training on graphic or web design and over the years have taught myself a wide range of things using mostly free software and online editors to achieve my goals. I use Microsoft Paint (a very basic program but one that you can do lots of simple things with) and GIMP (a free version of Photoshop) to do some more complicated and detailed photo edits. I also regularly employ online editors such as www.befunky.com which is great for creating collages, adding text, text outline, and things like that. There's a list of free editors in the **Resources** section at the end of this book.

Free websites are great when you are just starting out. They offer lots of customization, apps, widgets, and design options. However, just like the online editors, they are limited in what they can do and what they can offer.

When you are ready to take your author career and marketing to the next step, I recommend creating a paid author website which will give you more storage space, more bandwidth, and a much more professional looking domain name.

If you are not a tech savvy geek, have no fear, neither was I and I self taught myself everything I know about web design. Now all of my friends come to me when they need something designed online.

I would read online guides, watch video tutorials and honestly just use trial and error to design and text all design and function aspects of my site.

It takes a while to decode all the jargon too. Here's a basic breakdown of the components and functions of a website.

A **domain name** (custom URL) is the address and name of the store.

The **website** is like the interior space of a store, an area to explore content and products.

Bandwidth is the maximum occupancy (web traffic) allowed.

A **Hosting Server** and the website **storage space** is the actual drivespace on a company's hard drive that is dedicated to storing the information from your site and the functionality of its components.

A **landing page** is the register of the store that prompts a surfer to buy something. A landing page should have a call to action, asking the customer to do something (buy a product or sign up to an email list). The only thing you can do on a landing page is the call to action (other than close the window).

Conversion Rate is the amount of people who click a link, advertisement, or button vs. the amount of people who buy the product or sign up for the email subscription. Try testing different images and wording to see which yields a higher conversion rate (more sales or sign-ups.)

11

KINDLE DIRECT PUBLISHING

When you are published, head on over to Kindle (which you can do from the Createspace website dashboard) and upload a version of your book there. There are lots of guides and tips on formatting and uploading.

Enroll it in Kindle Direct Select. By doing so, you will open it up to many more readers. However you may not distribute an e-book version of you book anywhere else. Like ANYWHERE, its distribution must be exclusively on Kindle Direct Select, not ever on your personal site or blog.

The first perk is that you get 5 days (out of 90) to give your eBook away for free. *FREE?? Why would I want to do THAT!?* Giving books away for free is a way of marketing your book and getting it out there, you won't receive money for it at the time, but you have a chance of gaining some followers that otherwise may have never purchased or read your book in the first place. Once you have a loyal fan base, they will continue to purchase the books you put out.

You can always opt out at a later time, even if you have it selected to re-enroll you in the 90 day program. However, the exclusive rule is still in effect until the 90 days are up.

www.kdp.amazon.com

Amazon also has a **Look Inside** program where potential buyers can read an excerpt before buying your book. Whenever I'm in a book store, I always read the back cover and then the first page or three to see if I like the author's style. Style as well as content is a big influencer in whether or not I make the decision to purchase a physical book, so by enrolling it in Look Inside, online buyers can do that as well.

12

TAX & SMALL BUSINESS INFO

I know from my days as a door to door salesman (selling cable and internet packages) that when you only make money on commission (working for yourself) and not through an hourly rate (working for someone else) that you should set aside about 20% of what you make to pay towards taxes at the end of the year. Save the money and put it in a separate account so that you don't have to scrounge to gather the money come tax time.

If your business (book selling) is a sole proprietorship (and most authors are), then you get the Employer Identification Number in your name, not the business/imprint name. The IRS will only grant you one EIN for all the businesses you will ever operate. The businesses can have different names, but they use the same EIN.

You can have checks made to you

personally or to your business/imprint name. It's up to you. When you're a sole proprietor, you and the business are one entity for tax purposes.

Only if you form a corporation, will you get an EIN in the corporation's name. Most authors do not form corporations; it's overly complex for an author. Corporations just separate personal and commercial finances so one is not liable for the other.

While, I myself am no legal tax attorney, I did, however, complete a ten week long tax course from Liberty Tax Service in which I received a certificate of completion and a job offer in York, PA. So I'll happily relay everything that I know about the general topics. Just know that every county and state has different tax laws.

All personal income, whether it be from a nine to five job or writing professionally all goes into the same pot at the end of the year when filing your taxes. Subsequently, as long as you treat your writing as a business (with a clear intent to make a profit i.e., website, estore, business cards etc), you can deduct your business losses (where you spent more on producing a book i.e. designers, editors, etc. than what you made back in sales) from your overall gross (total) income.

However, most of us (although we WANT to make money off of it) do treat it as a hobby (as far as the IRS is concerned) because sales are here and there and not into the thousands of dollars yet. If this is the case, generally speaking, then all you would need to do is file that income under a 1099 form (miscellaneous income), and simply add it onto your gross income for the year. Createspace will issue you a 1099 to use when filing your taxes.

The rule of thumb when it comes to the IRS is that there is no such thing as too much documentation. Save every record documenting your expenses and time as a writer. Save receipts for actual goods or services that go towards your writing, thank you notes from schools, libraries, clubs, or conventions after doing readings or making an appearance. Acceptance and rejection letters from publishers. This all goes towards your credibility (not as a writer, but as someone that is trying to turn a profit and treat writing like a business). Keep invoices from books that you had printed. And keep these documents for at least three years although five to seven is much better and I'll tell you why.

I received a letter from my local tax bureau that they had not received tax filings from me for 2009 and 2010. Trying to remember back, I think I had spent most of my time in those years as a stay at home dad. So in 2014, I had to dig back and find records of any W-2s or jobs that I had worked in those two years. As it turns out, I earned a whopping $250.00 total for both years.

I had to create an account on www.ssa.gov, which keeps a record of all earnings reported under your social security number, in order to print off a W-2 from my employer. So save yourself some time and keep all your W-2s and tax documents in a physical or virtual filing cabinet. My fine for not having filed was under $2.00 and combined with late fees came out to be $11 and change. Good thing it hadn't been more.

Once you start selling a good number of books, it's a good idea to set up a business as an author by creating a DBA or "doing business as".

This is simply a fictitious business name that can be literally just about anything you want other than your own name but can include your name as well if you would want such as "Ryan Griffin Press" or "Griffin Enterprises".

It should definitely reflect whatever business you are in. The key to choosing a good business name is this: simple, straightforward, and original.

You cannot open a pizza business and call yourself Domino's even if you spell it differently. You would infringe on the likeness and good name of an already established company. If you are in the same field as a competitor with a similar name and it's close enough to cause confusion between your product and theirs, that's good enough for a lawsuit. Again, just avoid the possibility altogether and go with something more unique to your business.

Do not include the words "corp", "corporation" or "Inc." unless you are actually a corporation. That would be fraudulent advertising.

Look up other business names at www.uspto.gov which is the US Patent and Trademark Office.

Avoid using trademarked names of any corporate giants (basically anyone you would see a national commercial for on TV). While you may not be offering a similar product, these companies may sue you anyway just for using their likeness and staying out of the courtroom is the name of the game. You may have the best intentions in the world but being tied up in courtrooms and lawsuits for months or years on end is a just a drag on time and money for you.

Use search engines to look for similar business names and after you've found the right one, file a DBA or FBN (Fictitious Business Name) application in your county.

Once that is done, apply for a Reseller's Certificate. By sending a copy to Createspace, you will not have to pay sales tax on copies of your books that you buy to resell (assuming that you will pay the sales tax on the books that you sell yourself). You're going to give a good amount of books away for marketing purposes, do your best to keep records of books sold and books given away for tax purposes.

Every state and locality is different with its laws and licenses. Check out the Small Business Administration site www.sba.gov for useful info on applying for the correct permits and licenses.

In continuation, office supplies like envelops, stamps, business cards, flyers, bookmarks, posters etc are all tax deductible when you use them to support yourself as an author. Even portions of your laptop, car, and home can be a tax write off. Consult a tax expert in your county to figure out how much you can claim.

If you hire someone to design a contract or edit your book, **always** draw up and sign a contract and how much per service or hour their rates are. Most people are honest; contracts just help keep them that way. Be as specific as possible with the work that is being rendered, the cost of services, and the deadline or timeliness of such services as well.

If you pay someone more than $600 in a year, you're going to need to issue them a w2 form for the income. There are many sites that will give you free forms to use but you can pull them right off of the IRS website too. Go to www.irs.gov and do a site search for 1099 form (miscellaneous income) or simply ask them for a W-9 form (which will give you their social security or EIN). This helps them file taxes and can be deducted as a business expense for you. You only need to do this for an individual contractor, not a corporation.

If you decide to fundraise on a site like www.gofundme.com or www.indiegogo.com, you may ask for contributions or donations but be explicitly clear that they have no right to any percentage of your work or derivatives and that it is not a tax deductible donation. Usually saying that it goes towards or helps support the overall costs or operations of said project or business helps alleviate any legal liability. If you specifically ask for money to hire a cover designer and use that money for an editor instead, that constitutes fraud and you can be sued as well as charged and arrested.

Once you are established and fully immersed in the world of publishing and selling books, you're going to need to fully track expenses and income. There is lots of software out there to help you do this. Www.squareup.com is one source.

Factoid:
Seventeen of the top 100 Kindle
books in 2012 were self-published.
This number gets higher each year.

13

TIPS ON WRITING

Writing fiction is hard. Writing any type of book is hard but writing fiction is entirely from your imagination. With non fiction, you're just retelling what you already know (either your own story/knowledge or someone else's), just in your own way. So whilst I, myself, strive to become a fiction author, I want to share some of the great tips and tricks I've come across over the years, in hopes that it help you in becoming a great fiction author as well!

- George R. R. Martin (Game of Thrones) says that most authors are either a gardener or architect. The prior plants seeds of imagination and watches it grow while trying to shape it. The architect is someone who carefully scripts key plot points and chapter main points, possible endings etc. before sitting down to write.

- I've found that writing fiction is usually easier (for me) if I derive a chapter by chapter outline from the entire brainstorm of plot points and character points that I wrote down. I find that writer's block is less apt to happen when I already know what I'm going to write. If you know what is going to happen then you don't have to go back and rewrite something in to make the latter part of the book make sense (not as much anyway) and you usually avoid dead ends in your writing too. In a way, it's setting yourself up for success.

- Take a notebook, or create a document on your computer and list Chapter 1 through Chapter 20 (20 is an average count for a chapter book) and leave yourself about a paragraph's amount of space to write down the major things that are happening in each chapter. If you don't quite have 20 or even go way over, that's quite acceptable, but 20 gives you a good goal to shoot for while outlining your story. This strategy has absolutely helped me and I've come up with full chapter descriptions for an entire book in a single afternoon. Strive for a 40,000 word manuscript if you are aiming for a novel.

- Imagine you are writing a TV movie (2 hours long with commercial breaks). Each chapter is basically one segment before a commercial break. Notice how TV shows (or TV movies) leave off before a commercial break? With a mini-cliff hanger that makes you want to stick around! Use major cliff hangers (like TV shows do with the season finale) for different acts (an act in the Shakespearean sense) in your book or when ending your book to be continued in the sequel(s).

- Avoid generic titles like "The Girl", "The Boy", "The House" etc. Generic titles scream generic plots and characters!

- Write down notes about your story so you don't forget them. I have tons of notebooks, scrap pieces of paper, text messages, and emails to myself. I write down anything from a clever phrase my character would use, to a key plot point I want to make sure to include in my story. Authors have a million ideas, write the good ones down!

- Get a group of 3 to 5 (or more!) beta readers (people who proofread your work for errors in spelling, grammar, or continuity). Friends are sometimes more gentle than they are honest, so choose people you know will give you blunt and honest reviews. This isn't the time to stroke the ego, remove the ego altogether, and just focus on making your work better.

- It doesn't even occur to me if most people are not great typists since I learned how to type without looking at the keyboard in high school (which I recommend everyone learn how to do). I take the ability for granted but honestly, it helps SO much in your writing when you can move your fingers as fast as the words and ideas are coming to you. Not only that but computers are essentially an everyday use for most people (especially today's digital writers). Like learning Spanish, it's one of those skills that will never go to waste. See how fast you are here at www.typingtest.com or learn to become faster here at www.typingtrainer.com. Additionally you can use www.grammarly.com to improve grammar and punctuation (for free).

- "Don't tell me the moon is shining, show me the glint on a broken piece of glass." is one of my favorite pieces of advice for descriptive writing because it illustrates the difference between simply telling what is going on and showing it to the reader in a beautiful poetic way. Be descriptive but make sure you are adding to the tone and mood of your story and not taking away from it.

- People are emotional, not always logical. They do things spur of the moment for instant gratification which can be detrimental in the long term. Use this to create character conflict in the story.

- People feel compelled to do things, even though it may not have long term or direct effects.

- People act in their own self interest. Which means, generally, they cooperate in matters with others but when the stakes are great enough, they choose their own interests over what is best for everyone.

- People reveal their true selves when the chips are down, maybe someone shows how selfish they are when food or water runs out, etc. During these times, secondary (altruistic) characteristics like kindness or compassion (often times) fade away.

- People don't want to hear/see something unpleasant about someone or something they like. This is called "cognitive dissonance". When you admire something so much, you ignore any shortcomings, it happens in relationships, it happens with politicians, it happens with family members or idols.

- Balance character wants with needs. Like most people, it's not uncommon for these to be mutually exclusive. Desire: the big goal that propels the character forward. Need: the inner block or flaw that needs to be overcome.

- Every book needs a good log line. The Protagonist + the Antagonist + what's at stake = the log line. This is the overall premise or problem to draw in potential readers and buyers.

- For a good balance of long term and short term character or plot arcs, write the premise for three acts, and then write the premise for three mini-acts within each main act. Bring resolution to mini-acts after a few chapters; bring resolution to main acts towards the end of the book or roughly every $1/3^{rd}$ of the book.

- Practice causality: finish every action or decision. Bring them all to their logical conclusions; illustrate the consequences to all actions. Many actions have unforeseen outcomes. This is the law of Unintended Consequences.

- Story + Plot + Characters + Struggle move a story along, not what a character is wearing or what they had for lunch, unless it is essential to the plot (like a gasmask). Paint the beginning of the picture with descriptive language but let the reader finish it. Remember the story starts in your mind (the author) but has to finish in the mind of the reader. Let them use their imagination to finish the painting.

- Most people like to be funny (telling jokes, making fun of things) and helpful most of the time (helping someone carry something or offering advice). Realistic characters are not one sided.

- The main point of a story is to introduce a character, drive them up a tree, throw sticks and stones at them, and get them down safely (or if you truly must kill them, show how their death is poetic, ironic, necessary or like a martyr).

- The process is 30% writing and 70% editing, so just write. It's hard to know the meat of a thing unless you can look at the whole of it. If you keep editing and trying to perfect one scene, you could throw off the flow of the rest of the book. Write the big things (the main plot points, the main character arcs, the pitfalls, the resolutions, the ending) before trying to write the small things. It will help make writing scenes and dialogues easier.

- Show, don't tell. Use a characters POV and situation to narrate the story. Be brief; do not use 10 pages to explain 2 pages worth of material.

- Avoid clichés like the plague. I'm being ironic here but seriously do avoid using them. The reason people use these phrases is because people like to exaggerate and be popular. We use them because others use them. The problem is that they become over used and take value away from what we are trying to convey as writers because clichés wreak of unoriginality and being generic. I might have been okay with them as a teenager when I first started to broaden my taste in movies and books and they weren't so worn out but now I am at the age where I've seen the same clichés recycled so many times that it becomes a turn off to me as a consumer of such things. Beginner writers use a cliché to say something (that's why they all sound alike) and advanced writers find a new and unique way to convey an idea. Create your own simile. Authors that use really unique and original similes always impress me as a reader.

- Save often! I can't stress this enough. You never know when there will be a random power outage or your computer will crash. I've heard dozens of writers lament their luck over losing all of a work in progress. Get a thumb drive or online storage system to back up your work in case your computer crashes and is not salvageable. My desktop is probably 10 years old but I much prefer it to my laptop for large projects. I usually back up all my files onto a thumb drive once a month.

Factoid:

J.K. Rowling's real name is Joanne Rowling. She has no middle name. She picked the K from her family tree after her grandmother Kathleen, and chose the ambiguous name J.K. Rowling to publish, under the suggestion of her publisher citing the concern that being a female author writing about wizards might not help sales. It worked as she is one of the most successful authors of all time and most of her fan mail is addressed to "sir".

Resources

Free Publishing Sites
www.createspace.com - free publishing, print on demand service
www.kdp.amazon.com - Kindle Direct Publishing
www.smashwords.com - free publishing service
www.acx.com - turn your book into an audio book (Amazon, audible, itunes, low costs)
www.lightswitchpress.com - free publishing service
www.booktango.com - free publishing service
www.bookcountry.com - free publishing service
www.blurb.com - free publishing service, publish magazines too
www.ebookit.com - free publishing service

Writing/Reading sites
www.pw.org - Poets & Writers, find grants, contests, & more
www.medium.com - write and share stories with other writers
www.authorcentral.amazon.com - set up your Amazon Author page
www.goodreads.com - connect with readers
www.blogspot.com - free blog
www.wordpress.com - free blog
www.webs.com - free customizable site
www.wix.com - free customizable site
www.bluehost.com - fee based custom domain
www.linkedin.com - to market yourself professionally

as a writer

www.authorreach.com - 85 locations to submit your book for free

www.querytracker.net - keep track of which stores/agents etc you've contacted and connected with (for free)

www.agentquery.com (if you'd like an agent to help you land a publisher)

www.bookbub.com - fee based wide distribution network

www.draft2digital.com - percentage based distribution service

www.godaddy.com - to purchase a custom domain name

Cover Designers, Illustrators, & Free stock photos

www.selfpubbookcovers.com - over 9,000 book covers, most under $79.00

www.fiverr.com - all sorts of goods and services (including book covers) for starting at $5.00

www.bookdesigntemplates.com - for interior format templates

www.authormarketingclub.com - lots of services for authors including covers and advertising

www.thebookcoverdesigner.com - premade book covers

www.premade-bookcovers.com - exactly what you think

www.diybookcovers.com - do it yourself book cover design by Derek Murphy

www.damonza.com Book covers starting around

$500 (great for ideas for your book cover).
www.smashwords.com/list - for cover designers & formatters
www.facebook.com/digitialrevolutionimaging - low cost image editing service
www.vistaprint.com - design/print services
www.uprinting.com - design/print services
www.printerunner.com - design/print services
www.overnightprints.com - design/print services
www.canvasdiscount.com - canvas print service
www.unsplash.com - free stock images
www.pexels.com - free stock images
www.pixabay.com - free stock images
www.liberstock.com - search engine for free images
www.picjumbo.com - free stock images
www.tineye.com - perform reverse image searches

Photo Editing Sites & Free Font Sites
www.gimp.com - free software version of Photoshop
www.befunky.com - my favorite online picture editor
www.canva.com - free online picture editor
www.picmonkey.com - free online picture editor
www.1001fonts.com - free font downloads
www.myfonts.com - free font downloads
www.fontsquirrel.com - free font downloads
www.digitaldownload.io - free font downloads
www.creativindiecovers.com/free-online-isbn-barcode-generator - to add a price barcode to your ISBN barcode.
www.boxshot.com/3d-pack - to render your book in 3D.

Coaches, Pages, Groups, Communities to follow/join

www.thecreativepenn.com - Joanna (JF) Penn, Author coach

www.mandywallace.com - Mandy Wallace, Author tips

www.creativindie.com - Derek Murphy, author coach

www.brucethebookguy.blogspot.com - Bruce the Book Guy

www.thewritelife.com - The Write Life

www.writerscircle.com - The Writer's Circle

www.freedomwithwriting.com - Writing job postings

www.authorspublish.com - for weekly emails

www.authormarketingclub.com

www.librarything.com - book community

www.storycartel.com - Free books for honest reviews

www.wattpad.com - community for writers & readers

www.silverpenwriters.org - free peer review forum

www.scribophile.com - to share and critique works

www.meetup.com - to find others with similar interests in your area

www.facebook.com/groups/centralpalocalauthorsnetwork - Central PA Authors

Writing Professionally

www.inquisitr.com

www.Freedomfromwriting.com

www.thewritelife.com

www.beafreelancewriter.com

Tools for Writing

www.writersstore.com/scrivener - writing software

(for around $40)

www.writewellapp.com - free version of Scrivener

www.freeoffice.com - free version of Microsoft Office

www.openoffice.org - free office suite

www.libreoffice.org - free office suite

www.typingtest.com - see how many words per minute you can type

www.typingtrainer.com - learn to type faster here

www.grammarly.com - free grammar check

www.prowritingaid.com - free grammar check

www.hemingwayapp.com- free grammar check

www.topdf.com - free online PDF converter

www.freepdfconvert.com - free online PDF converter

www.sourceforge.net/projects/pdfcreator - free PDF software

www.bitly.com - Shorten any link down to just a few characters.

Additional Resources

www.copyright.gov - info on copyrights

www.loc.gov/publish/pcn - Pre-assigned Control Number Program

www.ssa.gov - records of personal earnings in past years

www.uspto.gov - US Patent and Trademark office

www.uspto.gov/trademarks - Trademark Electronic Search System

www.copyright.com - Copyright Clearance Center

www.govsimplified.co/ein/new/indiv - to apply for an EIN for a business

www.sba.gov - for info on small business licenses for

each state

www.myidentifiers.com - Bowker, to purchase ISBNS

www.creativecommons.org - Licensing forms

www.barcodegraphics.com - Barcode services

www.eff.org - Electronic Frontier Foundation

www.upwork.com - look for freelance editors and other professionals.

www.leadin.com - to start gathering email subscribers

www.pickfu.com - small fee based site for market research within minutes

www.helpareporter.com -aka HARO, for press releases

www.prnewswire.com/profnet - Pick the mind of an expert on whatever subject matter you are researching

www.sumome.com - free apps and buttons for your site

www.mailchimp.com - free email subscription service

www.aweber.com - fee based email subscription service

www.campaignmonitor.com - fee based email subscription service

www.constantcontact.com - fee based email subscription service

www.getresponse.com- fee based email subscription service

www.free-video-footage.com - free video blocks to use for a book trailer

www.addme.com - to monitor online sites that mention your name or book title

Acknowledgements

Thank you to everyone that has continued to support me through this amazing journey especially my mother who I owe the world to. I owe a big thanks to all of my favorite authors as a kid as well as some amazing teachers for having such an impact on me and sparking this love of writing. Thank you Michael Ferrara for your valuable feedback and constructive criticism!

If you enjoyed this book, please consider leaving a review on Amazon, Goodreads, or other online sites. If you think someone else could benefit from the information within, please share, recommend, or give this book as a gift. Thanks!

About the Author

Ryan has a voracious love for the craft of writing that goes all the way back to grade school. He dreamed of publishing for many years and finally found a professional and affordable way to do so with Createspace in 2015. He has a slew of fiction books that he would like to write but set to work on first writing *"How to Publish for Next to Nothing"* because he loves helping others and wanted to show them what he learned over the years.

He plans on starting an initiative in his community to get kids as well as aspiring writers of all ages involved with reading and writing. He firmly believes that if you can ignite someone's internal passion for the arts, that it will keep them out of trouble and focused on producing something they love, are proud of, and can share with the world.

If you would like to learn more about Ryan or his projects, follow him on

twitter @griffincyde
www.Facebook.com/AutumnShadowsPoetry
Or www.AutumnShadows.webs.com